Redouté to Warhol

BUNNY MELLON'S BOTANICAL ART

Redouté to Warhol

BUNNY MELLON'S BOTANICAL ART

Oak Spring Garden Foundation

New York Botanical Garden

Exhibition at The New York Botanical Garden
October 8, 2016 – February 12, 2017

© 2016 The New York Botanical Garden

The New York Botanical Garden
2900 Southern Blvd.
Bronx, NY 10458
nybg.org

All rights reserved. No part of this publication may be reproduced or transmitted in any form or by any means, electronic or mechanical, including photocopy, recording, or any other information storage and retrieval system, or otherwise without written permission from the publisher.

This catalog has been published on the occasion of the exhibition *Redouté to Warhol: Bunny Mellon's Botanical Art,* organized by The New York Botanical Garden, October 8, 2016–February 12, 2017.

Curators: Lucia Tongiorgi Tomasi, Tony Willis, Susan Fraser
Volume Editor: Joanna L. Groarke
Copy Editor: Sally Armstrong Leone
Design: The Graphics Office—Doug Clouse, Angela Voulangas

All works and photographs are reproduced courtesy of the creators and lenders of the material depicted. The following images are those for which separate or additional credits are due.

Cover: Georg Dionysius Ehret, [Southern magnolia] (detail), fig. 46
pp. 2-3: Charles Germain de Saint-Aubin, [Honeysuckle] (detail), fig. 6
fig. 4: Bridgeman Images
fig. 5: Horst P. Horst / *Vogue* © Condé Nast
fig. 7: Fred R. Conrad / *The New York Times* / Redux
fig. 9: Bettmann
fig. 10: Bridgeman Images
fig. 14: Fred R. Conrad / *The New York Times* / Redux
fig. 24: National Museum Wales / Bridgeman Images
fig. 27: Fred R. Conrad / *The New York Times* / Redux
figs. 47, 48: ©2016 Estate of Pablo Picasso / Artists Rights Society (ARS), New York
fig. 49: ©2016 The Andy Warhol Foundation for the Visual Arts, Inc./ Artists Rights Society (ARS), New York
p. 80: Fred R. Conrad / *The New York Times* / Redux

Published by The New York Botanical Garden

Printed in U.S.A.
ISBN 9780692783627

7
Foreword
GREGORY LONG

11
Introduction
SIR PETER CRANE, FRS

13
Acknowledgments

15
Bunny Mellon:
Her Life and Library
TONY WILLIS

29
Art & Nature
Libraries & Gardens
SUSAN FRASER

39
Bunny Mellon:
Collector and Gardener
LUCIA TONGIORGI TOMASI

70
Exhibition Checklist

80
Further Reading

P. Bessa.

FOREWORD

The study—and practice—of garden design and botanical art are two major activities of The New York Botanical Garden. For many years the Garden was fortunate to enjoy collaboration with the late Rachel Lambert "Bunny" Mellon. A trustee of The New York Botanical Garden in the late 1960s, Mrs. Mellon was an accomplished gardener and garden designer, and serious collector. Mrs. Mellon expanded our understanding of botanical art. Her generosity in sharing treasured objects from her collection for exhibitions throughout our decades of friendship has enriched our scholarship and touched the lives of thousands of visitors.

It is our great honor to host this exhibition of just a fraction of the masterworks housed in the Oak Spring Garden Library. *Redouté to Warhol: Bunny Mellon's Botanical Art* showcases some of the most important works in the art collection Mrs. Mellon assembled in the Library dedicated to botanical subjects she founded on the property of her estate in Upperville, Virginia. Over her entire lifetime, Mrs. Mellon collected more than

Figure 1
PANCRACE BESSA
[Pina cortadora], 1816–27
Watercolor on vellum with
gold border

16,000 works while simultaneously pursuing her horticultural interest in the estate's greenhouses and gardens, which she designed.

For their important contributions to the preparation of this exhibition, I wish to thank numerous individuals and organizations. Lucia Tongiorgi Tomasi, one of the world's preeminent scholars of herbals and botanical art, served as curator along with Tony Willis, Librarian of the Oak Spring Garden Library, and Susan Fraser, Vice President and Director of the LuEsther T. Mertz Library at The New York Botanical Garden. Their collaboration has resulted in this stunning exhibition. Amy Meyers, Director of the Yale Center for British Art, helped to arrange the loan of two paintings from its collection that were donated by Mr. and Mrs. Mellon, which greatly enhances the exhibition. The Oak Spring Garden Foundation, guided by Sir Peter Crane and William Robertson IV, has generously funded the exhibition.

The New York Botanical Garden is uniquely positioned to organize and present an exhibition celebrating the great range and breadth of Mrs. Mellon's collection. I hope you will be as inspired by the beauty and wonder of the plant world as was Mrs. Mellon herself.

GREGORY LONG
Chief Executive Officer
The William C. Steere Sr. President
The New York Botanical Garden

Figure 2
JOHANNA HELENA HEROLT, attrib.
[Crown imperial, scilla, and insects],
ca. 1695
Watercolor and bodycolor on vellum

INTRODUCTION

It was never my good fortune to know Rachel Lambert Mellon, but it is my privilege, every day, to be immersed in the environment she created at her estate in Upperville, Virginia. To be surrounded by her life's work is the greatest delight for anyone interested in the world of plants. Through the personality of her unique garden, and the exquisite taste expressed through her magnificent Library, Mrs. Mellon is ever present. It is our most sincere wish that if she were able to visit this exhibition at The New York Botanical Garden, curated with love by some of her closest friends, Mrs. Mellon would approve.

It is a singular honor for all of us at the Oak Spring Garden Foundation to play a role in helping to perpetuate and share Mrs. Mellon's gifts to the future, including her home, her garden, her library, and her estate. Our mandate is to use this remarkable legacy to serve the public interest—by facilitating scholarship, inspiring public dialog, and encouraging meaningful engagement with the history and future of plants—including especially their contributions to human well-being and significance in the culture of gardens and landscapes.

Figure 3
PIERRE-JOSEPH REDOUTÉ
[Tulips and roses] (detail), 1811
Watercolor on vellum

Through this exhibition, carried out in partnership with our close friends at The New York Botanical Garden, we have the pleasure of sharing the special qualities of the Oak Spring Garden Library with a broader audience. We are deeply grateful for this opportunity. Our hope is that all who visit the exhibition will enjoy this glimpse into Mrs. Mellon's unique domain—a world of great sensibility created by an inquiring mind that was always leavened with rarefied good taste.

This exhibition follows the continuum of human engagement with the world of plants that is embodied in Mrs. Mellon's collections. Her curiosity was all-encompassing, extending from the practice of cultivation, in which she was so deeply engaged in her own garden, to the capacity of plants to ignite the imagination, as reflected in the genius of artists as diverse as Jacques Le Moyne de Morgues and Sophie Grandval. In Mrs. Mellon's view of the world, the prescriptions of medieval herbalists and precise instructions on the pruning of fruit trees nestle comfortably alongside the exquisite artistry of anonymous medieval manuscript illuminators and the dazzling creativity of Pablo Picasso.

I am deeply grateful to all those who have worked so hard to create this exhibition, especially Gregory Long, Chief Executive Officer and The William C. Steere Sr. President of The New York Botanical Garden, and William Robertson IV, a long-time friend of the Mellon family, who initiated this project with the trustees of the Oak Spring Garden Foundation. I must also thank our inspired curators. Lucia Tongiorgi Tomasi, Professor at the University of Pisa, was not only a personal friend of Mrs. Mellon, but also worked closely with her in the production of two magnificent volumes—*An Oak Spring Flora* and *An Oak Spring Herbaria*—that feature selections from the Oak Spring Garden Library, including some of the treasures exhibited here. Tony Willis, Librarian at Oak Spring, and Susan Fraser, Vice President and Director of the LuEsther T. Mertz Library at The New York Botanical Garden, were also central to conceiving and creating this exhibition. We thank them all, as well as their dedicated colleagues at Oak Spring and in New York. The care and thought that everyone has invested in this exhibition, as their collective tribute to Mrs. Mellon, is plain for all to see.

SIR PETER CRANE, FRS
President
Oak Spring Garden Foundation

The New York Botanical Garden wishes to thank
the following individuals and institutions
for their assistance in the development of
Redouté to Warhol: Bunny Mellon's Botanical Art.

CURATORS

Lucia Tongiorgi Tomasi
Tony Willis
Susan Fraser

OAK SPRING GARDEN LIBRARY

Ronnie Caison
Nancy Collins
Randy Embrey and gardeners
Kimberley Fisher
Jim Morris
Ricky Willis
Gloria Woodson

YALE CENTER FOR BRITISH ART

Amy Meyers, *Director*

FUNDERS

Oak Spring Garden Foundation

Exhibitions in the Mertz Library
are made possible by the
LuEsther T. Mertz Charitable Trust.

BUNNY MELLON: HER LIFE AND LIBRARY

Tony Willis

Rachel Lambert Mellon was born in New York City at 777 Madison Avenue on August 9, 1910. Today that address is 45 East 66th Street, now an architectural landmark. More than a century later, Mrs. Mellon's legacy, in the form of a select group of her most cherished treasures, lives on in the city of her birth for an honorary exhibition at The New York Botanical Garden. The location could not be more appropriate. Mrs Mellon admired and respected the Botanical Garden for its educational and vocational programs that serve a broad public. These extraordinary artworks, many being shown publicly for the first time, were very much a part of Mrs Mellon's daily life in Upperville, Virginia.

Early Inspiration

Born into a prominent family, Mrs. Mellon's childhood years were spent in Princeton, New Jersey, on her family's estate, Albemarle. She was the eldest of Gerard Barnes Lambert (1886-1967) and Rachel Parkhill Lowe Lambert's (1889-1974) three children. She was called "Bunny" from birth, a nickname given by her nurse.

Figure 4
SOPHIE GRANDVAL
Dandelion, 1990
Oil on canvas

Her father and her maternal grandfather, Arthur Houghton Lowe (1853-1932), gave the young Rachel an exposure to art and books that had a profound effect throughout her life. Both were not only astute businessmen, but also erudite collectors. Lambert, head of Warner-Lambert Pharmaceutical Company, had amassed a library of maps, sailing literature, and architecture books and prints. He authored three books: *Yankee in England*, two editions, (1937 and 1939), *Murder in Newport* (1938), and *All Out of Step: A Personal Chronicle* (1956). Lowe established several textile mills in Massachusetts and Alabama. He introduced his enthusiastic granddaughter to Transcendentalism and the wonders of the natural world. Their positive influences, along with her innate talent and artistic sensibilities, helped Rachel to establish her unique sense of style and elegance.

Famous childhood classics by authors such as Maurice Boutet de Monvel, Edmund Dulac, Kate Greenaway, H. Willebeeck Le Mair, and Arthur Rackham sparked in Rachel a passionate interest in learning about and creating gardens. Her father allotted a large square space at the family estate in New Jersey for her early gardening experiments. There her imagination and ideas on gardens and gardening became a reality. While planning and maintaining her new garden, 12-year-old Rachel observed the famous Olmsted Brothers from Boston, who were working at that time on the grounds. Of this period in her life, she would later remark, "I feel I was born at the right time, this country was younger and people from all walks of life were working hard for a better future. There was a sense of pride and unity, and I had my books, drawing pads, supplies, and gardening paraphernalia. This gave me a sense of stability which in turn helped me throughout my life."

Mrs. Mellon's lifelong penchant for purchasing rare books and manuscripts derived from her need for reference materials to support her interests. She took some of these works with her when she went to board at Foxcroft School in Middleburg, Virginia, in the early 1920s. There she designed a small garden for Charlotte Haxall Noland (1883-1969), founder and president of the school. For every project during her long and active life, Mrs. Mellon always referred to her personal library. She often remarked that rare books on plants and garden plans, especially French or Italian works, were her most important early guides. She would frequently say, "A library is built during a lifetime; it doesn't happen overnight."

Figure 5
Bunny Mellon as photographed for *Vogue*, 1965

Figure 6
CHARLES GERMAIN DE SAINT-AUBIN
[Honeysuckle]
Watercolor, pen and ink
in *Receu l de plantes copiées d'aprés nature par de Saint Aubin, dessinateur du Roy Louis XV*, 1736–85

(previous) Figure 7
JAN VAN KESSEL THE ELDER
[Study of plants, insects, arachnids, mollusks, and reptiles] (detail), 1653–58
Oil on copper

Figure 8
Watercolor sketch of a garden scene by the young Bunny Lambert, ca. 1932

A Career in Gardening

At 18 Rachel helped her father design and maintain the grounds and gardens at his new estate, Carter Hall, in Millwood, Virginia. During her first marriage from 1932 to 1948 to Stacy Barcroft Lloyd, Jr. (1908–94), she oversaw the construction of Apple Hill, their home with gardens and a greenhouse at Carter Hall. In 1935 Rachel and Stacy purchased *The Clarke Courier*, a local newspaper based in Berryville, Virginia. Stacy was an editor and Rachel wrote a gardening column.

In addition to her family commissions during this same period, one of Rachel's first jobs in 1933 was designing a garden in New Jersey for Hattie Carnegie (1880-1956), the famous fashion icon who was based in New York City. During a visit to Hattie's salon, the two ladies worked out a deal— a garden in exchange for a dress and coat. Thus the industrious Rachel embarked on a decades-long career designing private and public gardens, which she continued to pursue following her marriage to Paul Mellon (1907–99) in 1948, all the while collecting rare books and art in search of knowledge about her favorite subjects of garden design, horticulture, natural history, and botanical art.

Figure 9
The White House Rose Garden, as designed by Bunny Mellon, with magnolias and tulips in full bloom in April, 1963

Mrs. Mellon's most famous commissions were the design of two iconic gardens at the White House. Following a 1961 meeting with President John F. Kennedy (1917–63), she redesigned the Rose Garden, adjacent to the West Wing. The Jacqueline Kennedy Garden was opened in 1965 by Lady Bird Johnson (1912–2007) in honor of the former First Lady. This garden occupies a complementary position on the East side of the White House Residence portico. Both remain today, and are actively used for White House events, including ceremonies and press conferences.

After President Kennedy's assassination, Mrs. Mellon was asked by Mrs. Kennedy to assist in the design of the President's gravesite in Arlington National Cemetery. She collaborated with landscape architect Perry Wheeler (1913–89) and John Carl Warnecke and Associates, a consulting firm based in Washington, D.C. Mrs. Mellon was instrumental in selecting and purchasing the West Falmouth granite and millstones used to construct the grave. She also helped with the design and placement of the eternal flame and selected plants, including the dogwoods and saucer magnolias.

In the 1970s, Mrs. Mellon consulted with architect I. M. Pei (b. 1917) on the design of the grounds surrounding the John F. Kennedy Presidential Library and Museum in Boston. Of their collaboration, Pei remarked, "Mrs. Mellon has the combination of sensitivity and imagery with technical knowledge that you only find among the best professionals."[1] During this same period, she worked

[1] Paula Deitz, "The Private World of a Great Gardener," *The New York Times*, June 3, 1982.

with landscape architect Dan Kiley (1912–2004) on plans for the landscaping surrounding the National Gallery of Art in Washington, D.C.

Throughout her career, Mrs. Mellon designed gardens for personal friends as well. Her clients included Jean Schlumberger in New York City; Jacqueline Kennedy Onassis on Martha's Vineyard; and Charles Ryskamp in Princeton. Each garden was thoroughly planned, with the goal of creating a distinct design for that particular individual. She generally favored native trees and plants in her design, and required that trees be beautifully pruned, creating focal points within the garden.

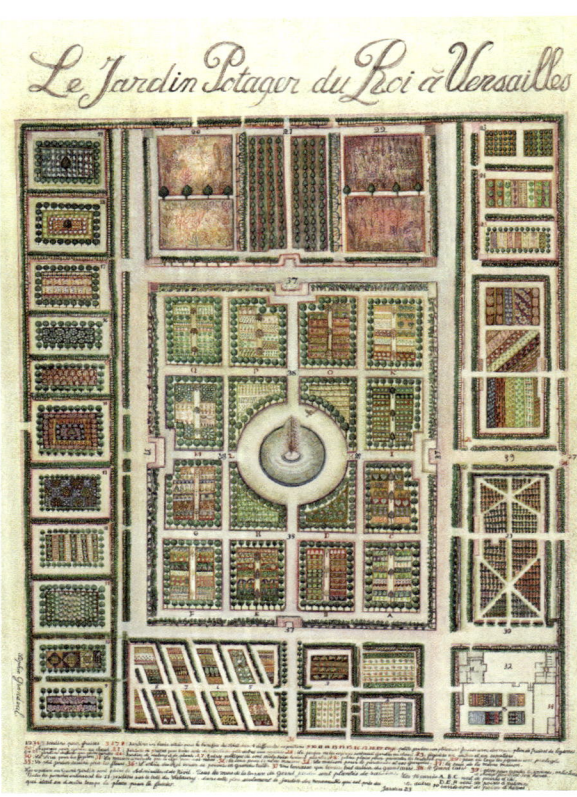

Figure 10
SOPHIE GRANDVAL
Potager du Roi, Versailles
ink and watercolor on paper

Figure 11
FRANÇOIS DE GEEST
[Poppies]
Bodycolor on vellum
in *Jardin de rares et curieux fleurs faictes pr. François de Geest de Leovarde en Frise*, ca. 1660

2
Françoise Mohrt, *The Givenchy Style* (New York: Vendome Press, 1998), 9.

Mrs. Mellon's close friend Hubert de Givenchy once wrote, "Bunny Mellon…is a perfectionist. Her gardens are enchanting and her houses refined…I have learned much from her, and I am infinitely grateful."[2] In the 1990s, Givenchy sought her advice on restoring the *Potager du Roi,* the vegetable garden created for Louis XIV during the 17th century at Versailles. During this four-year endeavor, Mrs. Mellon's personal library was an invaluable resource. By studying her numerous editions of *Instruction pour les jardins fruitiers et potagers* by Jean-Baptiste de La Quintinie (1626–88), the king's head gardener, and with much help from the World Monuments Fund, Mrs. Mellon and Givenchy were successful in returning the garden to its original glory. For her efforts, Mrs. Mellon was awarded the *Ordes des Arts et des Lettres* medallion by the French government in 1995.

Oak Spring Garden Library

In the early 1970s at a social function in Pittsburgh, Mrs. Mellon was asked about her library. She responded she didn't have a specific library building or a single space dedicated to her books, but that they were unfortunately scattered about in many locations. The conversation inspired Paul Mellon to help her construct a separate building to house her exquisite collection.

In spring 1976, Mrs. Mellon began to work diligently with New York City-based architect Edward Larrabee Barnes (1915-2004). Together they drafted architectural plans for a new library, and soon after, construction began. The building was completed in spring 1981. Mrs. Mellon's vast collections of natural history, horticulture, and botany were moved *en masse* to this new building, which she named the Oak Spring Garden Library. Two decades later, another wing was designed for expansion purposes with the help of local architect Thomas Beach, from Earth Design Associates. The annex was completed in winter 1997.

Papaver spinosum   *Papaver Rhaas*

Pap. corniculatum

Figure 12
JACQUES LE MOYNE DE MORGUES,
attrib.
[Arum with butterfly]
Watercolor on vellum
in [An album of flowers and fruit],
late 1500s

Figure 13
JACOB MARREL
Semper Augustus
Watercolor on paper
in [Tulpenboek], *Jacobus Marrellus Franckendalensis delineavit ad vivam,…*,
1642

Today the Oak Spring Garden Library is a thriving research center housing 16,000 objects: books, both modern and rare; manuscripts; drawings and prints; and sculpture. All are available for scholarly research and study. The collection encompasses horticulture and landscape design, botany, natural history, voyages and travels, herbs and herbals, trees, flowers, fruits and fruit trees, architecture, decorative arts, and classical literature (poetry, short stories, novels, etc). Four discursive catalogs have been published: *An Oak Spring Sylva* (history of trees and tree cultivation, 1989), *An Oak Spring Pomona* (history of fruit and fruit trees, 1990), *An Oak Spring Flora* (history of flowers and their iconography, 1997), and *An Oak Spring Herbaria* (history of herbs and herbals, 2009).

When Mrs. Mellon passed away in March 2014, an era had come to an end. Today more is being written regarding her private life; however, her legacy lives on through her Library and its diverse collection. In an article that appeared in *Vogue* in 1965, Mrs. Mellon wrote, "Too much should not be explained about a garden. Its greatest reality is not reality, for a garden, hovering always in a state of becoming, sums its own past and its future. A garden, like a library, is a whole made up of separate interests and mysteries."[3] Our hope is that all who see this exhibition and its many botanical riches will be inspired by Mrs. Mellon's extraordinary foresight in collecting and interest in gardens and botanical art.

TONY WILLIS is Librarian at Oak Spring Garden Library.

[3] Rachel Lambert Mellon, "Green Flowers and Herb Trees," *Vogue*, December 1965.

Figure 14
Bunny Mellon in the
Oak Spring Garden Library, May 1982

ART & NATURE
LIBRARIES & GARDENS

Susan Fraser

It has been my pleasure to visit the Oak Spring Garden Library and work alongside co-curators Lucia Tongiorgi Tomasi and Tony Willis to select some of the extraordinary pieces of botanical art that epitomize Mrs. Mellon's vocation to horticulture, botany, and landscape design. It is this common interest that brings these works to The New York Botanical Garden and we are delighted to be the host venue for this exhibition.

Mrs. Mellon's association with The New York Botanical Garden extends back to 1967 when she was elected to the Board of the Garden. She served on the Grounds Committee from 1968 to 1970. Works from her collection have been part of several other exhibitions in the LuEsther T. Mertz Library, specifically *Flowers by Redouté: Artist for an Empire* (2005), *Georg Ehret: The Greatest Botanical Artist of the 1700s* (2009), and *The Renaissance Herbal* (2013). It is again our privilege to

Figure 15
JACQUES-GUILLAUME VAN BLARENBERGHE
LOUIS-NICOLAS VAN BLARENBERGHE
[Frontispiece]
Watercolor and bodycolor on paper
in *Horti herbarii Domini Lamberti Michaelis Winckelman (Dum Viveret) Pharmacopolae Lillensis et Botanophili…*, 1755

SARRACENIA *foliis gibbis*. Hort. Cliff.

exhibit some of the treasures that speak to the connoisseurship and sensibilities of a collector whose exceptional aesthetic formed the Oak Spring Garden Library collection. Many of the works selected for *Redouté to Warhol: Bunny Mellon's Botanical Art* fall outside the classical canon of botanical art, but encompass Mrs. Mellon's erudite and wide-ranging interest in the natural world. The curators selected works that focus, in particular, on the unique and rare botanical, floral, and decorative arts in the collection. A concerted effort was made not to select published works or treatises that may also be held in the Mertz Library or other botanical, horticultural, or academic libraries.

These works provide a marvelous complement to the Mertz Library, which was built over 125 years as a vast resource for scholars and students alike. The Oak Spring Garden Library and the Mertz Library each contain a treasure trove of knowledge embedded in the rare and beautiful books and objects housed within them, yet profound differences are apparent. The latter is situated in the heart of the Garden, and occupies the 6th floor of the LuEsther T. Mertz Library Building. At its core, the Mertz Library is a collection of collections—libraries acquired from the collections of botanical or horticultural personalities such as Garden co-founders Nathaniel Lord Britton and Elizabeth Knight Britton, Elgin Botanic Garden founder David Hosack, renowned botanist John Torrey, Czech pharmacologist Emil Starkenstein, and contemporaries of Mrs. Mellon such as Dr. David L. Andrews and Elizabeth Kals Reilley. Like Mrs. Mellon, these collectors had a passion for books, plants, and gardens, and understood the fundamental importance of preserving our botanical heritage. The Mertz Library serves as an oasis of botanical knowledge in the center of an urban environment, where access to collections dating to the 12th century as well as to hundreds of electronic databases facilitate both historical as well as cutting-edge research.

In contrast, the Oak Spring Garden Library is immersed in the Virginia landscape in an airy building designed to allow unobstructed interchange between inside and outside. There is a lovely casualness about the Oak Spring Garden Library where researchers encounter books on open shelves and atop tables, still-life paintings on the walls, modern art alongside Renaissance works and decorative objects with depictions of the natural world, creating the idyllic environment in which Mrs. Mellon was able to indulge her own quest for knowledge. Like the Mertz Library, Mrs. Mellon's collecting interest also spanned several centuries and included works from medieval to modern, "blending the past with the present and future."[1]

This exhibition showcases exemplars from the thousands of pieces of art, dating from the 14th to the 20th centuries, from drawings made before the invention of the printing press to floral works made by artists for the French royal court and produced for the Sun King, Louis XIV; from Renaissance works on canvas and exquisite botanical paintings on vellum to 19th-century scientific models and modern lithographs on paper, which Mrs. Mellon collected over her lifetime.

Figure 16
GEORG DIONYSIUS EHRET
Sarracenia foliis gibbis, 1764
Watercolor and bodycolor on vellum

Figure 17
ELIZABETH BLACKWELL
[Turnip], ca. 1735–36
Watercolor on paper

1
Rachel Lambert Mellon, foreword to *An Oak Spring Herbaria,* by Lucia Tongiorgi Tomasi (Upperville, Virginia: Oak Spring Garden Library, 2009), xxii.

Figure 18
JAN BAPTISTA VAN FORNENBURGH
[Still life with flowers, insects, and a lizard], 17th century
Oil on wood

(top) Figure 19
KONRAD VON MEGENBERG
[Plants]
Manuscript text and watercolor
on paper
in *Buch der natur*, ca. 1350

Figure 20
[Plants]
Hand-colored woodcut
in *Hye nach volget das puch der natur*
by Konrad von Megenberg
Augsburg: Hanns Bümler, 1475
LuEsther T. Mertz Library,
The New York Botanical Garden

A manuscript copy of the famous *Buch der Natur* by Konrad von Megenberg (1309–74), a prolific writer best known for this popular encyclopedia of natural history and medicine, is the earliest work shown in the exhibition [fig. 19]. The work is a survey of all known natural history at the time, and contains chapters on the nature of man, astronomy and meteorology, zoology, botany, mineralogy, metal, and water. While Mrs. Mellon's herbal is a unique manuscript created around 1350, the Mertz Library holds a rare copy of the first printed version—an incunabulum—printed in 1475, before the invention of movable type [fig. 20]. Through our collaboration on this exhibition, we are fortunate to be able to show these two exceptional volumes side-by-side. Created more than 100 years apart, they provide a compelling comparison of some of the first known depictions of plants in books, with Latin descriptions of their uses.

Figure 21
PANCRACE BESSA
[Virginia spiderwort], 1816–27
Watercolor on vellum with gold border

The Mertz Library holds many published works that contain the artwork of famous botanical personalities such as Nicolas Robert, Pierre-Joseph Redouté, Elizabeth Blackwell, and Pancrace Bessa. Blackwell is best known for the publication *A Curious Herbal*, which was published between 1737 and 1739 containing 500 copperplate engravings from drawings she made of medicinal plants growing at the Chelsea Physic Garden. The popularity of the publication merited several editions. Mrs. Mellon purchased 72 of Blackwell's original watercolor drawings notable for their sketch-like quality [fig. 22]. Similiarly, Pancrace Bessa, one of Pierre-Joseph Redouté's most talented students, made hundreds of drawings for *Herbier general de l'amateur,* an eight-volume set containing 575 illustrations of ornamental plants compiled by Jean Claude Michel Mordant de Launay [fig. 21]. This set of drawings on vellum, outlined in gold leaf, was commissioned by order of Charles X of France as a 1826 New Year's gift for the Duchess of Berry. The Duchess later presented this collection to her sister, Teresa Christiana, wife of the Brazilian emperor Dom Pedro II, who took the drawings to South America. Over time they had been purchased from the estate of the former director of the Botanical Garden in Rio de Janeiro and in 1946 they were brought to New York and exhibited at The New York Botanical Garden. From a historical viewpoint, the study of these original works along with their provenance and the associated printed work can reveal much about the transmission of knowledge about plants throughout the world.

Figure 22
ELIZABETH BLACKWELL
[Wood strawberry], ca. 1735–36
Watercolor on paper

Mrs. Mellon's own scholarly pursuits are evident in the publications produced by the Oak Spring Garden Library that carefully document and describe many of the works contained in the Library with a focus on flowers, trees, fruit, and herbals. *An Oak Spring Sylva*

(1989), *An Oak Spring Pomona* (1990), *An Oak Spring Flora* (1997), and *An Oak Spring Herbaria* (2009) are indispensable works on the history and bibliography of many of the most important botanical works ever produced and are a resource used by librarians and scholars worldwide. It is heartening to know that Mrs. Mellon was committed to sharing her extraordinary collection as part of her continuing legacy. The Oak Spring Garden Library is a trove of botanical heritage waiting to be explored. Like the LuEsther T. Mertz Library, home of the Humanities Institute (funded by The Andrew W. Mellon Foundation), it is a place where scholars and professionals conducting their own research can share ideas, make meaningful connections, and pursue innovative, interdisciplinary approaches to the study of the history of botanical art, plant exploration, garden and landscape design and history, and the study of plants and society.

As Mrs. Mellon noted, "Countless imaginative creations have found their expression in flowers, and the cycle of their life has the strength of sensual pleasure with their scent, fruit, and seeds. Their presence inspires our tired spirit with their fragile being, and allows our minds to go beyond its earthly limits. Poets and lovers wander into their secret realms, hoping for permission to share part of their mystery."[2] In this exhibition, we share nearly 80 of those inspired creations.

SUSAN FRASER is Vice President and Director of the LuEsther T. Mertz Library at The New York Botanical Garden.

2
Rachel Lambert Mellon, foreword to *An Oak Spring Flora*, by Lucia Tongiorgi Tomasi (Upperville, Virginia: Oak Spring Garden Library, 1997), xxv–xxvi.

Figure 23
HENRI ROUSSEAU (Le Douanier)
Flowers of Poetry, 1890–95
Oil on canvas

BUNNY MELLON: COLLECTOR AND GARDENER

Lucia Tongiorgi Tomasi

"Years of collecting brought with it new ideas and new friends that have built a life for me beyond the Garden Library's walls, and opened unexpected doors,"[1] Rachel "Bunny" Mellon wrote in *An Oak Spring Flora*, one of two volumes that I had the honor and the pleasure to write for her and with her, on some of the treasures in her Library of rare manuscripts and books, prints, drawings, paintings, and artifacts conserved at Oak Spring in Upperville, Virginia. My time working there was one of the richest and most intellectually stimulating periods in my life as a scholar.

Bunny's Private Realm

Though she consciously led an inconspicuous life, Bunny Mellon was an individual of great originality who in her quiet way exerted considerable influence on contemporary culture. Her collection was guided by precise objectives and unerring taste born of an acute sensibility that led her to identify some of the most significant works in the history of botany and botanical art—not only the most beautiful but also those of

Figure 24
AUGUSTUS EDWIN JOHN
Dorelia in the Garden at Alderney Manor, Dorset, ca. 1911
Oil on panel
Yale Center for British Art,
Paul Mellon Collection

[1] Rachel Lambert Mellon, foreword to *An Oak Spring Flora*, by Lucia Tongiorgi Tomasi (Upperville, Virginia: Oak Spring Garden Library, 1997), xxvii.

the greatest historical and cultural importance—at a time when the study of these subjects was still only of tangential interest to most scholars. Her unique collection served as a resource for researchers and was admired by her many friends, among them Hubert de Givenchy, Audrey Hepburn, Frank Langella, and Jacqueline Kennedy.

Bunny's qualities as a collector were enhanced by her intellectual curiosity and her awareness of the natural world. Throughout her life she was drawn to the beauty found in the harmonious convergence of art, science, and nature, whose endless variety never ceased to amaze and delight her. Her passion for gardening extended to cultivation of plants and flowers (particularly wildflowers), horticulture, and agriculture. Her equally deep interest in garden design and history and botanical art and landscape painting produced through the centuries provided inspiration for her gardening activities. She was always eager to learn new methods of cultivation and to "get her hands dirty" in the most mundane gardening tasks, and was also deeply appreciative of the most profound meanings contained in the artworks in her collection.

The Oak Spring Garden Library's unusual surroundings and rare holdings set it apart from other collections and reflect Bunny's unique understanding of the relationship between nature and culture. Her Library was her private realm, and it remains a magical place in which every corner evokes her presence. Visitors to the Library are immediately charmed by the breadth and variety of her collection—medieval manuscripts with bejeweled covers, extraordinary drawings by Pierre-Joseph Redouté, and unusual *objets d'art*—all chosen with infallible taste.

As Bunny recounted to me on several occasions, she was inspired to begin collecting books at the precocious age of ten, when she first saw 12 engravings from *The Flower Garden Display'd*, a catalog by London nurseryman Robert Furber (1674–1756) in 1734. She was so struck by the exuberant flower compositions that she subsequently acquired several fine editions herself. Another work that later had a great impact on her as a gardener was the three-volume treatise on horticulture published in Paris in 1821, *Le jardin fruitier* by Louis Claude Noisette (1772–1849), gardener to the Count of Provence, the future king, Louis XVIII. His elegant *planches* depict "espaliers and cordons" and *treillages* created out of painstakingly trained fruit trees. Bunny chose to reproduce one of these on the cover of *An Oak Spring Pomona,* one of several compendia of the works in her collection [fig. 26]. She even re-created several of the espaliers designed by Noisette at Oak Spring, an exercise that she was most felicitously called upon to repeat when invited to restore the *Potager du Roi* at Versailles in the 1990s.

The Oak Spring Garden Library can be reached from Bunny's stately country house by passing through the garden, which is modeled on a medieval *hortus conclusus* in combination with an English kitchen garden. In this space Bunny brought to fruition many of the ideas she encountered in the books in her collection. Like her

Figure 25
PIERRE-JOSEPH REDOUTÉ
[Carnations, double hyacinth, and bellflower], 1812
Watercolor on vellum

Figure 26
Engraving of an espalier in *Le jardin fruitier* (1821) by Louis Claude Noisette. This was a favorite resource for Bunny Mellon, whose garden included many fruit trees.

Figure 27
Bunny Mellon working in her garden
of espaliered fruit trees, May 1982

Library, Bunny's garden breathes refinement, and at each turn one comes upon unexpected details that were tended by Bunny with a knowing eye in her quest to model nature without altering it. Her love of art, books, and gardening was probably most aptly captured in the central domed room of her greenhouse, which was decorated with *trompe l'oeil* frescoes by French artist Fernand Renard (b. 1912). These paintings captured the essence of Bunny's daily life through depictions of the myriad objects she loved: baskets, fruits and flowers, garden tools, and books.

The Exhibition
It was not an easy matter for the curators of this exhibition to select a sampling from the wealth of works of art in the Oak Spring Garden Library that faithfully reflects Bunny's unique personality. *Redouté to Warhol: Bunny Mellon's Botanical Art* does not focus on Bunny's exceptional printed herbals and books, many of which can also be found in The New York Botanical Garden's LuEsther T. Mertz Library. Instead it features unique and rare individual works, ranging from unpublished manuscripts to modern paintings and objects of great personal significance. It fittingly opens with a painting by Welsh artist Augustus Edwin John, *Dorelia in the Garden at Alderney Manor* [fig. 24]. She was greatly attached to this work, which hung for many years in her bedroom. The simple view of a young woman leaning thoughtfully on a staff in her garden evokes the life Bunny led at Oak Spring, and serves as an appropriate introduction to the exhibition, which celebrates the vision of one of the world's great collectors and her deep personal connection to nature.

Medieval Arts and Science
The earliest works in Bunny's collection include a rare manuscript copy of *Buch der Natur*, 14th-century German *magister* Konrad von Megenberg's comprehensive encyclopedia of the natural world [fig. 19]. The original manuscript, the first natural history text in the German language, is especially fascinating when compared to a 1475 incunabulum of the same work that is held in the Mertz Library [fig. 20]. Both are illustrated with simple yet delightful drawings of plants, animals, and other subjects pertaining to natural history. Drawn from nature, the illustrations in both versions were meant to serve as a practical resource for doctors and scientists.

Bunny's collection also includes illuminated manuscripts from the 15th century. Books of hours, miniature illustrated compendia of prayers and Bible verses, were used by their aristocratic owners during private devotions. One especially fine example is attributed to the great Ghent-born artist Simon Bening, who was considered to be among the most accomplished painters of miniatures in all of Europe. It contains a page in which the central image of St. Catherine of Alexandria is framed by motifs from the natural world: flowers, fruits, and insects so lifelike they might just have been plucked from a garden and gently pinned on the page [fig. 28]. Another book of hours, by an unknown artist of the early decades of the century,

Figure 28
SIMON BENING, attrib.
[Saint Catherine of Alexandria]
Manuscript text and bodycolor
on vellum
in *Horae Beatae Mariae
Virginis ad usum Romanum*, 1524

depicts the Flight into Egypt surrounded by intricately detailed vegetal patterns that include exquisite gold illumination. While not strictly botanical art, these works are examples of the importance of natural and plant motifs in early European art.

Figure 29
JACQUES LE MOYNE DE MORGUES
[Grapes and apricots]
Hand-colored woodcut
in *La clef des champs*, 1586

Figure 30
JACQUES LE MOYNE DE MORGUES
A Young Daughter of the Picts,
ca. 1585
Watercolor and gouache,
touched with gold on parchment
Yale Center for British Art,
Paul Mellon Collection

The Art of Florilegia

The 17th century was a period of rapid, pivotal change in the fields of botany and horticulture in Europe. Plantsmen were fascinated by the new species that were arriving from distant lands as a result of worldwide exploration and trade, and by new cultivated plants being produced by horticulturists through skillful hybridization. The "florimania" that gripped the continent during this period was documented in collections of botanical illustrations known as florilegia as well as floral still lives. Bunny collected many distinguished works from this period.

The diversity of engagement with floral subjects in early Renaissance Europe is perhaps best illustrated by the differences between the work of Jacques Le Moyne de Morgues and Girolamo Pini. Le Moyne made important contributions to the study of botany as well as to the genre of botanical illustration. His activity took him from France to England, and even to the peninsula of Florida in the New World, which he visited as a member of the expedition of the Huguenot explorer René Goulaine de Laudonnière (ca. 1529-74). In his watercolor and gouache drawing *A Young Daughter of the Picts* [fig. 30], Le Moyne reinterprets a young maiden of the ancient Scottish tribespeople as a damsel of the New World. The exhibition also features a manuscript album with paintings of common flowers and fruits [fig. 12] and a rare volume of woodcut engravings (one of three known extant copies) [fig. 29]. Titled *La clef des champs*, meaning "key to nature," this work served as a pattern book for embroiderers and other artisans.

In contrast, two canvases by Pini, a Tuscan painter who flourished during the first decade of the 17th century, are very different [figs. 31, 32]. In each panel the artist has arranged a series of rare horticultural and exotic species against a dark background in an elegant composition complete with a *trompe l'oeil* cartouche inscribed with their common names. While Le Moyne's work documents plants he encountered close to home, Pini focused instead on the newly available imports and exotic bulbs. This portrayal of both the foreign and the local appealed to Bunny.

Figure 31
GIROLAMO PINI
[Flowers with a fritillary in the center],
ca. 1612
Oil on canvas

Figure 32
GIROLAMO PINI
[Flowers with an iris in the center],
1612
Oil on canvas

The passion for gardens, flowers, new species, and botanical illustration at the court of the Sun King, Louis XIV, is documented in the splendid *Theatrum florae*. Published in Paris by Daniel Rabel, botanical painter to the king's brother, the duke Gaston d'Orléans, this volume is highly unusual. The illustrations were hand-colored by a relatively unknown artist—Guillelmus Théodorus—who was so secure in his talent that he proudly signed the title page [fig. 33]. A richly detailed, realistic garden scene by the Flemish artist Jacques Guillaume Blarenberghe and his son Louis-Nicolas served as the frontispiece to a voluminous florilegium dedicated to the plant collection in Lille of the 18th-century pharmacist Lambert Michael Winckelman [fig. 15]. Intended as an herbal of native and exotic plants, this superb work was devoted to "all lovers of botany," as stated in the preface. It was unfinished at the time of Winckelman's death, thus, the bound volume in Bunny's collection contains only some of the paintings.

The panorama of 17th-century European botanical studies is further represented in this exhibition by fine manuscripts on vellum featuring plants drawn from life, including a work by Domenico Buonvicini, a little-known but talented Venetian artist. He embellished the first page of his herbal with images of a Persian buttercup, lily-of-the-valley, statice, and Mexican poppy [fig. 34]. *Jardin de rares et curieux fleurs*, a work by the skilled Flemish artist François de Geest, features poppies with unusual double blooms [fig. 11]. Another manuscript, made by German artist Hans Simon Holtzbecker, is different from traditional botanical illustrations because it depicts cut flowers, thornapples, that appear to be intended more as ornamental than scientific drawings [fig. 35]. Nicolas Robert, *peintre ordinaire du Roi pour la miniature*, was another accomplished 17th-century artist who specialized in the genre of flower painting. His renditions of flowering plants on vellum are genuine masterpieces in which the transparent veils of color of the flower petals and the supple quality of their stems and leaves have been rendered with virtuoso realism [fig. 36].

Figure 33
GUILLELMUS THÉODORUS
[Title page]
Hand-colored engraving
in *Theatrum florae*
by Daniel Rabel (1578–1637)
Paris: N. de Mathonière, ca. 1622–24

Figure 34
DOMENICO BUONVICINI
[Flowers]
Watercolor and bodycolor on vellum
in [An album of plants], 1601

Figure 35
HANS SIMON HOLTZBECKER
[Thornapples]
Bodycolor on vellum
in [An album of plants], ca. 1665

Figure 36
NICOLAS ROBERT
[Tulip, bellflower, and sunflower], n.d.
Watercolor on vellum with gold border

Figure 37
DANIEL SEGHERS
[Flower bouquet in a glass vase], n.d.
Oil on copper

Dutch Tulipomania

Bunny Mellon took an interest in the phenomenon of tulipomania that convulsed Holland in the 1630s. She acquired a collection of catalogs, books, pamphlets, and paintings that demonstrate how the rapid inflation in price of rare tulip bulbs, which peaked in the years from 1634 to 1637, seized the imaginations of artists of the day.

Extraordinarily detailed botanical drawings were produced by German still-life painter Jacob Marrel for various *Tulpenboeken*, catalogs of plates of unusual varieties that were used by nurserymen and horticulturists to entice the discriminating collector. Exquisite examples of the commercial arts of the period, these straightforward views of the plants were intended to showcase flower forms and colors. They were bound into books often containing handwritten lists of rare bulbs with their prices, and served a very practical purpose [figs. 13, 38, 55]. Yet another perspective on this historical period is offered by the famous engraving after a drawing by Pieter Nolpe, *Floraes Gecks-Kap.* This broadside illustrates the social and economic consequences of the unbridled speculation associated with the tulip trade, as described in cautionary detail in the lengthy caption [fig. 39]. Two still lifes—one by Jan Baptista van Fornenburgh and the other by Daniel Seghers—feature the exotic bulbous plant. Seghers chose to focus on the spectacular opulence of the flower, in this case a variety with flaming scarlet petals [fig. 37]. While van Fornenburgh has imbued his work with symbolic connotations, weaving a butterfly, a fly, a lizard, and water dripping from a crack in the stone table into his composition, all allusions to the transitory nature of life—and presumably the fleeting nature of earthly riches [fig. 18].

Figure 38
JACOB MARREL
Vice-Roy
Watercolor on paper
in [Tulpenboek], *Jacobus Marrellus Franckendalensis delineavit ad vivam,…*, 1642

Figure 39
PIETER NOLPE
Floraes Gecks-Kap of Afbeeldinge van't wonderlijcke Jaer van 1637 doen d'eene Geck d'ander uytbroeyde, de Luy Rijck sonder goet, en Wijs sonder verstant waeren, 1637
Engraving and etching on paper

Cabinet of Curiosities

Another fascinating glimpse of Holland during its Golden Age is provided by 17 meticulously detailed paintings on copper by Jan van Kessel the Elder. Still in their original frames, the works depict flowers, insects, caterpillars, spiders, reptiles, and a snail [fig. 41]. Van Kessel, who specialized in small works of natural subjects such as these, sometimes painted outdoors from life, which accounts for his exquisitely detailed images. Works like these were often displayed together in a grid, and might even have been set into furniture designed for the display of collections of natural objects and curiosities. This set of works by van Kessel would have been a prized item in any 17th-century collection, as they were in Bunny's.

Figure 40
GERARD VAN SPAENDONCK
[Dahlias]
Black chalk on paper
in [An album of flower studies], n.d.

Figure 41
JAN VAN KESSEL THE ELDER
[Studies of plants, insects, arachnids, mollusks, and reptiles], 1653–58
Oil on copper

Painters of the French Court

As the 17th century drew to a close, Paris gradually overtook Holland as the European center for flower painters. Dutch artist Gerard van Spaendonck became *peintre du Roi* in France and a co-founder of the Académie des Beaux-Arts, where he trained many prominent French artists of this period. Van Spaendonck was greatly admired and his opulent floral still life paintings were sought after during his lifetime by Parisian intellectuals and connoisseurs. Bunny collected two albums of van Spaendonck's drawings and three additional works. A chalk sketch of a dahlia from a very rare album by the artist stands

out vividly with its naturalistic realism and elegance [fig. 40]. Van Spaendonck's most famous student, Pierre-Joseph Redouté, is known today as one of the world's most celebrated botanical artists. A drawing of *Dodecatheon meadia*, a North American plant that was first described by English naturalist Mark Catesby, could strictly be termed a botanical illustration [fig. 42]. In contrast, a very elegant work featuring a bellflower, a hyacinth, and carnations clearly privileges artistic aims over the scientific [fig. 25]. Redouté was the favorite artist of Napoleon Bonaparte's first wife, Joséphine Beauharnais, herself a lover of art and flowers, who, like Bunny, was a great collector.

Bunny was a true connoisseur of French art of the 18th and 19th centuries, which occupied a privileged place in her Library. Other important French artists represented by superb works in the collection include Claude Aubriet, who succeeded Daniel Rabel and Nicolas Robert as *peintre du Roi pour la miniature* for the French court. Aubriet contributed many splendid botanical drawings to the collection of *vélins* at the Jardin des Plantes in Paris. More intimate but no less interesting is the manuscript entitled *Receuil de plantes* by Charles Germain de Saint-Aubin, an artist who belonged to a dynasty of engravers, embroiderers, and painters engaged in service to the French monarchy. This unique collection consisting of more than 250 watercolors and sketches, some with handwritten notes, was regarded as a visual diary of the artist's life, showing his interest in experimenting with various techniques and styles, and even in creating fanciful images of imaginary plants. Saint-Aubin's fertile imagination is attested to by a plate depicting a honeysuckle blossom protruding from a rolled-up print, which seems to be set atop a page listing the physical attributes of the plant [fig. 6].

Masters of Botanical Art

Bunny collected works as much for their historical importance as for their stunning beauty. Her collection was not bound by a period in time or an artistic style, but it features a large number of works by some of the most well-known artists of the 18th and 19th centuries, considered by many scholars to be the height of the field of botanical art. She always displayed these works alongside lesser-known yet equally talented artists of the period, and viewed them with the same interest for what they reveal about the world of plants.

Figure 42
PIERRE-JOSEPH REDOUTÉ
Dodecatheon meadia, 1793
Watercolor, pen and ink on wove paper

Figure 43
MARIA SIBYLLA MERIAN
[Tulip tree and two butterflies],
ca. 690
Watercolor on vellum

Figure 44
BARBARA REGINA DIETZSCH
[Two quinces on a branch], n.d.
Bodycolor on paper

Figure 45
PANCRACE BESSA
[Citrus], 1816–27
Watercolor on vellum with gold border

Figure 46
GEORG DIONYSIUS EHRET
[Southern magnolia], ca. 1737
Bodycolor on vellum

Maria Sibylla Merian began her artistic career with training by her stepfather, Jacob Marrel. Her richly detailed watercolor drawings of plants and insects firmly place her among the greatest botanical artists of her time. A drawing of a tulip tree branch with two butterflies reveals her unparallelled ability to depict the natural world with an artistic eye as well [fig. 43]. She tutored her daughters—Johanna Helena and Dorothea Maria Henrietta—in the art of scientific illustration, and both later became her collaborators. An exquisite work attributed to Johanna Helena Herolt, likely based on a drawing by her mother, features the luxurious blooms of crown imperial and scilla depicted with extreme accuracy [fig. 2].

Barbara Regina Dietzsch also belonged to a family that had produced many painters, and she herself was a celebrated botanical and zoological artist working in 18th-century Nürnberg, though she is less widely known today. Bunny owned two of her works: a beautiful plate of a hellebore and a bodycolor drawing of two quinces [fig. 44]. As was typical in Dietzsch's works, the quince branch with its ample fruit stands out against a dark background in a striking rendition of a fragment of nature. Unlike Merian or Dietzsch, Elizabeth Blackwell was not the product of an artistic dynasty. It was out of sheer economic necessity—in order to extract her husband from debtors' prison—that she produced the plates for her *A Curious Herbal*, which depicted medicinal plants drawn from specimens in the Chelsea Physic Garden in London [figs. 17, 22].

Many striking works by one of the most renowned botanical painters of the 18th century, German artist Georg Dionysius Ehret, are included in Bunny's collection. Ehret collaborated for a time with Carl Linnaeus, Swedish naturalist and author of the binomial system of nomenclature. In a magnificent painting of southern magnolia, Ehret combines his virtuoso skill as a botanical illustrator with the analytical eye of a scientist, capturing the palpable qualities of the flowering branch with its leaves, buds, and fruiting pod in a complex and polished composition [fig. 46].

Far less well-known than Ehret, Baldassare Cattrani was a botanist and artist from Rome who during the course of his career worked for the Botanical Garden of Padua and for Joséphine Beauharnais in the garden at her Paris chateau, Malmaison. Bunny's collection includes several of his works, such as a fine botanical painting of *Ipomea heterophylla*, a member of the morning glory family, whose supple stem and blue flowers have been arranged in an elegant composition. Pancrace Bessa, another great and prolific natural history artist and student of van Spaendonck, was known for his detailed and delicate portrayals of botanical specimens and his superb engraving technique. During his lifetime, his work won him such fame that the Duchess of Berry, the daughter-in-law of the king of France, Charles X, became one of Bessa's most loyal patrons, and summoned him to give painting lessons to members of her family. Bunny purchased 90 of the preparatory plates drawn on vellum by the artist for *Herbier général de l'amateur* (1816–27), [figs. 1, 21, 45] a serial publication on flowering plants by Mordant de Launay and Loiseleur Deslongchamps that had been commissioned by King Charles X himself.

Figure 47
(left) PABLO PICASSO
Pot of Flowers I, 1957
Colored lithograph with crayon

Figure 48
(right) PABLO PICASSO
Pot of Flowers II, 1958
Colored lithograph with crayon

Figure 49
(opposite) ANDY WARHOL
Vine Leaf Marinade, 1959
Ink and watercolor on paper

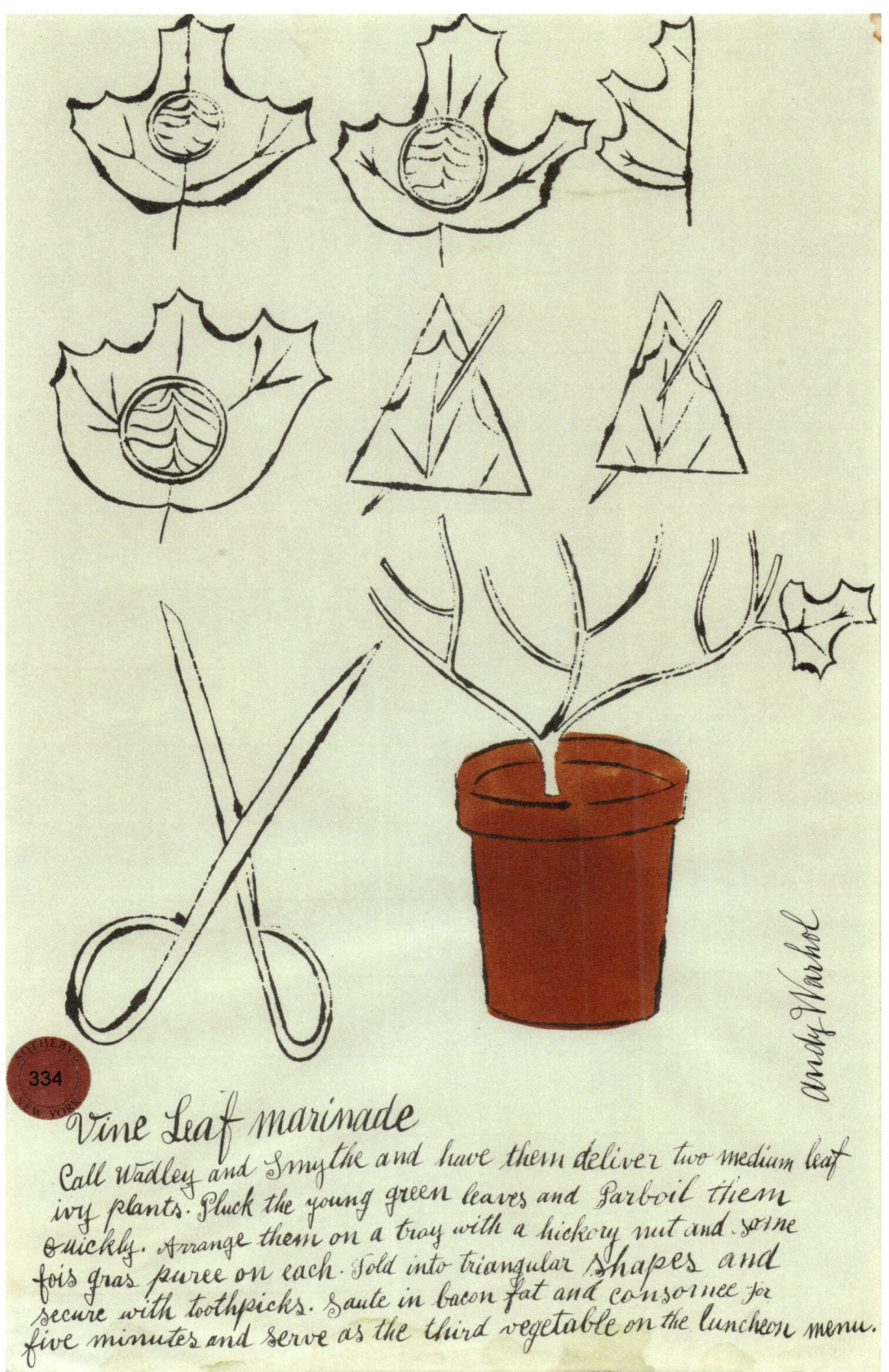

Vine Leaf Marinade

Call Wadley and Smythe and have them deliver two medium leaf ivy plants. Pluck the young green leaves and parboil them quickly. Arrange them on a tray with a hickory nut and some fois gras puree on each. Fold into triangular shapes and secure with toothpicks. Saute in bacon fat and consommee for five minutes and serve as the third vegetable on the luncheon menu.

(previous) Figure 50
[Jars of botanical pomades and creams]
Hand-colored engraving, watercolor and bodycolor on paper
in *Dépôt de la crème du cathay de Jean-Marie Farina, distillateur de la véritable eau de cologne*
Paris: Jean-Marie Farina Company, ca. 1815–20

Flowers and Plants in Modern Art

Works of more recent artists are also represented in the exhibition. A still life of violas and other humble garden plants painted at the end of the 19th century by Henri Rousseau in the intense, glowing colors typical of his palette and a monumental depiction of a dandelion painted a century later by Sophie Grandval provide an artistic perspective on some of the more unassuming garden plants that Bunny appreciated [figs. 23, 4]. Just as she collected the works of masters of botanical art, which often celebrated the curious and rare in meticulous detail, she also found pleasure in more abstract depictions of nature's more mundane offerings. Pablo Picasso's colored lithographs of potted plants with additions in crayon attest to this, while Andy Warhol's depiction of a grape leaf accompanied by a fanciful recipe shows Mrs. Mellon's appreciation for more playful engagements with botanical subjects [figs. 47, 48, 49]. A floral sketch on a box top by Eliza Lloyd Moore, Bunny's daughter, demonstrates how Bunny's fascination with art and nature influenced members of her family [fig. 59].

Objets de Vertu

Bunny's library contained many *objets d'art* and curios. Some were her own acquisitions and others were gifts from those who knew of her great love for all things botanical. Among them are tiny, bejeweled flower arrangements in the style of Peter Carl Fabergé; boxes decorated with floral motifs; and minuscule books on subjects pertaining to flowers and gardens. A charming *papier mâché* model of a female melon flower, one of several in her collection made by skilled artisans in Berlin during the first quarter of the 19th century, could be disassembled to show its various parts and was used for demonstration purposes in botany classes. Particularly enchanting is a rare catalog dating to the same period that was produced by the eponymous Paris perfumery, Jean-Marie Farina, which was founded by the grandson of the inventor of cologne water [fig. 50]. The company's exclusive line of soaps, creams, and perfumes, most of them made from floral essences, are depicted in elegant watercolors. These objects illustrate the breadth of her collection and the wide range of works that engage with botanical subjects.

During my career I have spent many weeks at the Oak Spring Garden Library, consulting the collection and writing on the works. I often saw Bunny pause to contemplate an intimate still life by Italian artist Cristoforo Munari [fig. 51]. The work features arranged citrus fruits and some pieces of blue-and-white porcelain—two of Bunny's favorite motifs—in a restrained composition brightened by the use of enamel-like colors. She acquired this painting in 1988, and enjoyed it for the remainder of her life, returning to it again and again with fresh curiosity and interest. This work, like all those

assembled for this exhibition, offers insight into a truly extraordinary individual, a collector and gardener whose impact on the history of gardens and on botanical and horticultural studies was quietly profound. The product of her life's work, Bunny Mellon's collection of botanical art will continue to educate and inspire future generations of scholars and gardeners who visit the Oak Spring Garden Library. Her own description of her collection summarizes perfectly why her influence will endure:

> This collection of books and drawings grew as a way of life, not just a gathering of rare and interesting books bought at the enticement of an enthusiastic bookseller, but chosen one by one for their special and unusual contents and design, as well as their relationship to books already part of the collection. It is a working library where mystery, fascination, and romance contribute to centuries of the art of gardening as a source of discovery.[2]

Figure 51
CRISTOFORO MUNARI
[Still life with a quince, an apple, lemons, and three Chinese blue-and-white cups], ca. 1700
Oil on canvas

LUCIA TONGIORGI TOMASI is former full professor of the history of art at the Università di Pisa. A prolific writer, Dr. Tomasi focuses on the relationships among art, science, gardens, and nature.

Translated from Italian by Lisa Chien

[2] Rachel Lambert Mellon, preface to *An Oak Spring Garland*, by Sandra Raphael (Upperville, Virginia: Oak Spring Garden Library, 1989), 5.

EXHIBITION CHECKLIST

Figure 52

Figure 53

Figure 24
AUGUSTUS EDWIN JOHN
(Welsh, 1878–1961)
Dorelia in the Garden at Alderney Manor, Dorset, ca. 1911
Oil on panel
Yale Center for British Art,
Paul Mellon Collection

Medieval Arts and Science

Figure 19
KONRAD VON MEGENBERG
(German, 1309–74)
[Plants]
Manuscript text and watercolor on paper
in *Buch der natur*, ca. 1350

Figure 20
[Plants]
Hand-colored woodcut
in *Hye nach volget das puch der natur*
by Konrad von Megenberg (1309–74)
Augsburg: Hanns Bümler, 1475
LuEsther T. Mertz Library,
The New York Botanical Garden

Figure 52
Unknown artist
(Bourges)
[Flight into Egypt]
Manuscript text and bodycolor with
gold illumination on vellum
in *Horae Beatae Mariae Virginis Secundum Usum Ecclesiae Romanae*, ca. 1400–51

Figure 28
SIMON BENING, attrib.
(Flemish, 1483/84–1561)
[Saint Catherine of Alexandria]
Manuscript text and bodycolor on vellum
in *Horae Beatae Mariae Virginis ad usum Romanum*, 1524

The Art of Florilegia

Figure 53
NICOLAS ROBERT
(French, 1614–85)
[Scilla], n.d.
Watercolor and bodycolor on vellum
with gold border

Figure 36
NICOLAS ROBERT
(French, 1614–85)
[Tulip, bellflower, and sunflower], n.d.
Watercolor on vellum with gold border

Figure 34
DOMENICO BUONVICINI
(Italian, active second half 16th–
first half 17th century)
[Flowers]
Watercolor and bodycolor on vellum
in [An album of plants], 1601

Figure 33
GUILLELMUS THÉODORUS
(French, ca. early 17th century)
[Title page]
Hand-colored engraving
in *Theatrum florae*
by Daniel Rabel (1578–1637)
Paris: N. de Mathonière, ca. 1622–24

Figure 11
FRANÇOIS DE GEEST
(Dutch, ca. 1639–99)
[Poppies]
Bodycolor on vellum
in *Jardin de rares et curieux fleurs faictes pr. François de Geest de Leovarde en Frise*, ca. 1660

Figure 35
HANS SIMON HOLTZBECKER
(German, ca. 1649–71)
[Thornapples]
Bodycolor on vellum
in [An album of plants], ca. 1665

Figure 15
JACQUES-GUILLAUME VAN BLARENBERGHE
(Flemish, 1679–1742)
LOUIS-NICOLAS VAN BLARENBERGHE
(Flemish, 1716–94)
[Frontispiece]
Watercolor and bodycolor on paper
in *Horti herbarii Domini Lamberti Michaelis Winckelman (Dum Viveret) Pharmacopolae Lillensis et Botanophili…*, 1755

Figure 30
JACQUES LE MOYNE DE MORGUES
(French, ca. 1533–before 1588)
A Young Daughter of the Picts, ca. 1585
Watercolor and gouache, touched with gold
on parchment
Yale Center for British Art,
Paul Mellon Collection

Figure 29
JACQUES LE MOYNE DE MORGUES
(French, ca. 1533–before 1588)
[Grapes and apricots]
Hand-colored woodcut
in *La clef des champs*, 1586

Figure 12
JACQUES LE MOYNE DE MORGUES, attrib.
(French, ca. 1533–before 1588)
[Arum with butterfly]
Watercolor on vellum
in [An album of flowers and fruit], late 1500s

Figure 31
GIROLAMO PINI
(Italian, active 1610–20)
[Flowers with a fritillary in the center], ca. 1612
Oil on canvas

Figure 32
GIROLAMO PINI
(Italian, active 1610–20)
[Flowers with an iris in the center], 1612
Oil on canvas

Dutch Tulipomania

Figure 18
JAN BAPTISTA VAN FORNENBURGH
(Dutch, 1585–ca. 1649)
[Still life with flowers, insects, and a lizard],
17th century
Oil on wood

Figure 37
DANIEL SEGHERS
(Flemish, 1590–1661)
[Flower bouquet in a glass vase], n.d.
Oil on copper

Figure 54

Figure 39
PIETER NOLPE
(Dutch, ca. 1613–53)
Floraes Gecks-Kap of Afbeeldinge van't wonderlijcke Jaer van 1637 doen d'eene Geck d'ander uytbroeyde, de Luy Rijck sonder goet, en Wijs sonder verstant waeren, 1637
Engraving and etching on paper

Figure 54
JACOB MARREL
(German, 1614–81)
Geel en root van Leyden
Watercolor on vellum
in [Tulpenboek], 1634

Figure 13
JACOB MARREL
(German, 1614–81)
Semper Augustus
Watercolor on paper
in [Tulpenboek], *Jacobus Marrellus Franckendalensis delineavit ad vivam,...*, 1642

Figure 38
JACOB MARREL
(German, 1614–81)
Vice-Roy
Watercolor on paper
in [Tulpenboek], *Jacobus Marrellus Franckendalensis delineavit ad vivam,...*, 1642

Figure 55
JACOB MARREL
(German, 1614–81)
Vroege Nonswit
Watercolor on paper
in [Tulpenboek], *Jacobus Marrellus Franckendalensis delineavit ad vivam,...*, 1642

Figure 56
JACOB MARREL
(German, 1614–81)
Register van negenen negentig soorten der beroemste Tulpanen...
Folio, manuscript text
in [Tulpenboek], *Jacobus Marrellus Franckendalensis delineavit ad vivam,...*, 1642

Figure 55

Figure 56

Figure 57

Cabinet of Curiosities

Figure 41
JAN VAN KESSEL THE ELDER
(Flemish, 1626–79)
[Studies of plants, insects, arachnids, mollusks, and reptiles], 1653–58
Oil on copper

Painters of the French Court

Figure 3
PIERRE-JOSEPH REDOUTÉ
(Belgian, 1759–1840)
[Tulips and roses], 1811
Watercolor on vellum

Figure 25
PIERRE-JOSEPH REDOUTÉ
(Belgian, 1759–1840)
[Carnations, double hyacinth, and bellflower], 1812
Watercolor on vellum

Figure 42
PIERRE-JOSEPH REDOUTÉ
(Belgian, 1759–1840)
Dodecatheon meadia, 1793
Watercolor, pen and ink on wove paper

Figure 40
GERARD VAN SPAENDONCK
(Dutch, 1746–1822)
[Dahlias]
Black chalk on paper
in [An album of flower studies], n.d.

Figure 6
CHARLES GERMAIN DE SAINT-AUBIN
(French, 1721–86)
[Honeysuckle]
Watercolor, pen and ink
in *Receuil de plantes copiées d'aprés nature par de Saint Aubin, dessinateur du Roy Louis XV*, 1736–85

Figure 57
CLAUDE AUBRIET
(French, ca. 1665–1742)
Cacao
Watercolor and bodycolor on vellum
with gold border
in *Papillons, plantes, fleurs et animaux, peints par Aubriet*, ca. 1725

Masters of Botanical Art

Figure 16
GEORG DIONYSIUS EHRET
(German, 1708–70)
Sarracenia foliis gibbis, 1764
Watercolor and bodycolor on vellum

Figure 46
GEORG DIONYSIUS EHRET
(German, 1708–70)
[Southern magnolia], ca. 1737
Bodycolor on vellum

Figure 58
BALDASSARE CATTRANI
(Italian, late 18th–early 19th century)
Ipomea heterophylla, ca. 1799
Watercolor on vellum

Figure 58

Figure 59

Figure 43
MARIA SIBYLLA MERIAN
(German, 1647–1717)
[Tulip tree and two butterflies], ca. 1690
Watercolor on vellum

Figure 2
JOHANNA HELENA HEROLT, attrib.
(Dutch, 1668–after 1721)
[Crown imperial, scilla, and insects], ca. 1695
Watercolor and bodycolor on vellum

Figure 44
BARBARA REGINA DIETZSCH
(German, 1706–83)
[Two quinces on a branch], n.d.
Bodycolor on paper

Figure 17
ELIZABETH BLACKWELL
(Scottish, ca. 1700–58)
[Turnip], ca. 1735–36
Watercolor on paper

Figure 22
ELIZABETH BLACKWELL
(Scottish, ca. 1700–58)
[Wood strawberry], ca. 1735–36
Watercolor on paper

Figure 45
PANCRACE BESSA
(French, 1772–1846)
[Citrus], 1816–27
Watercolor on vellum with gold border

Figure 21
PANCRACE BESSA
(French, 1772–1846)
[Virginia spiderwort], 1816–27
Watercolor on vellum with gold border

Figure 1
PANCRACE BESSA
(French, 1772–1846)
[Pina cortadora], 1816–27
Watercolor on vellum with gold border

Flowers and Plants in Modern Art

Figure 23
HENRI ROUSSEAU (Le Douanier)
(French, 1844–1910)
Flowers of Poetry, 1890–95
Oil on canvas

Figure 60

Figure 47
PABLO PICASSO
(Spanish, 1881–1973)
Pot of Flowers I, 1957
Colored lithograph with crayon

Figure 48
PABLO PICASSO
(Spanish, 1881–1973)
Pot of Flowers II, 1958
Colored lithograph with crayon

Figure 49
ANDY WARHOL
(American, 1928–87)
Vine Leaf Marinade, 1959
Ink and watercolor on paper

Figure 4
SOPHIE GRANDVAL
(French, b. 1936)
Dandelion, 1990
Oil on canvas

Figure 59
ELIZA LLOYD MOORE
(American, 1942–2008)
[Box top with flower drawings], n.d.
Pencil and watercolor on cardboard

Objets de Vertu

Figure 50
[Jars of botanical pomades and creams]
Hand-colored engraving, watercolor and bodycolor on paper
in *Dépôt de la crème du cathay de Jean-Marie Farina, distillateur de la véritable eau de cologne*
Paris: Jean-Marie Farina Company, ca. 1815–20

Figure 60
CRISPIJN VAN DE PASSE
(Dutch, ca. 1594–1670)
[Putto watering a garden]
Engraving
in *Emblemata Amatoria by Georgius Albertus Camerarius*
Venetiis: Ex Typographia Sarcinea, 1627

[Citrus plant], ca. 1910–15
Gold stem, nephrite leaves, orange enamel fruit, white enamel flower blossom and bud, small diamond in center of blossom, in crystal vase in the style of Peter Carl Fabergé

Figure 62
[Dandelion], ca. 1910–15
Gold stem, nephrite leaves, diamond seed centers with asbestos fibers, in crystal vase in the style of Peter Carl Fabergé

[Raspberry], ca. 1910–15
Gold stem, nephrite leaves, rhodonite fruit, in crystal vase in the style of Peter Carl Fabergé

Figure 61
[Botanical model of a melon blossom]
Papier-mâché
Berlin, R. Brendel Studio, early 19th century

[Apothecary bottles], n.d.
Cobalt blue glass

[Decorative box with French gardens], n.d.
Engraved and hand-colored

Figure 61

[Box with inscription "Rachel L. Lambert August 9, 1915"], n.d.
Silver

[Decorative box with fruit vignettes], n.d.
Enamel and gold

Figure 51
CRISTOFORO MUNARI
(Italian, 1667–1720)
[Still life with a quince, an apple, lemons, and three Chinese blue-and-white cups], ca. 1700
Oil on canvas

Figure 62

FURTHER READING

Deitz, Paula. "The Private World of a Great Gardener." *The New York Times,* June 3, 1982.

Filler, Martin. "Oak Spring Splendors." *House Beautiful*, vol. 1 (140): June 1998.

Mellon, Rachel Lambert. "Green Flowers and Herb Trees." *Vogue,* vol. 146 (10): December 1965.

_____. "The Jacqueline Kennedy Garden." *House and Garden*, vol. 156 (10): October 1984.

_____. "Mrs. Mellon's Secret Garden." *House and Garden,* vol. 160 (6): June 1988.

_____. "The White House Rose Garden." *House and Garden*, vol. 156 (9): September 1984.

Moss, Charlotte. "The Elegant World of Bunny Mellon." *Flower,* vol. 9 (2): March/April 2015.

_____. "The Eloquence of Silence." *The New York Times Style Magazine,* June 15, 2014.

Raphael, Sandra. *An Oak Spring Garland: Illustrated Books, Prints, and Drawings from the Oak Spring Garden Library, Upperville, Virginia*. Catalog published in association with the exhibition held in the Leonard L. Milberg Gallery for the Graphic Arts, Princeton University Library. Upperville, Virginia: Oak Spring Garden Library, 1989.

_____. *An Oak Spring Pomona: A Selection of the Rare Books on Fruit in the Oak Spring Garden Library*. Upperville, Virginia: Oak Spring Garden Library, 1990.

_____. *An Oak Spring Sylva: A Selection of the Rare Books on Trees in the Oak Spring Garden Library*. Upperville, Virginia: Oak Spring Garden Library, 1989.

Reginato, James. "Bunny Mellon's Secret Garden." *Vanity Fair*, no. 600: August 2010.

Ridgway, Christopher. "A Garden Furnished with Books." *Country Life*, vol. CXCI, no. 51/52: December 18-25, 1997: 36-41.

_____. "To Walk in a Vision of Economy and Grace." *Country Life,* vol. CXCII, no. 1: January 1, 1998: 30-35.

Tomasi, Lucia Tongiorgi. *An Oak Spring Flora: Flower Illustration from the Fifteenth Century to the Present Time: A Selection of the Rare Books, Manuscripts, and Works of Art in the Collection of Rachel Lambert Mellon*. Upperville, Virginia: Oak Spring Garden Library, 1997.

_____. *An Oak Spring Herbaria: Herbs and Herbals from the Fourteenth to the Nineteenth Centuries: A Selection of the Rare Books, Manuscripts, and Works of Art in the Collection of Rachel Lambert Mellon*. Upperville, Virginia: Oak Spring Garden Library, 2009.

_____. *The Renaissance Herbal*. Catalog published in association with the exhibition held in the William D. Rondina and Giovanni Foroni LoFaro Gallery, LuEsther T. Mertz Library at The New York Botanical Garden. Bronx, N.Y.: The New York Botanical Garden, 2013.